Into Nature We Go

Nicole Lea Turner

ISBN 979-8-88832-428-8 (paperback)
ISBN 979-8-88832-430-1 (hardcover)
ISBN 979-8-88832-429-5 (digital)

Christian Faith Publishing
832 Park Avenue
Meadville, PA 16335
www.christianfaithpublishing.com

Printed in the United States of America

A book for children everywhere to encourage
venturing out and exploring nature.

Nicole Lea Turner

Presented to:

____

From:

____

Date:

____

To my husband Tom and little Wyatt for making this possible

In every walk with nature, one receives far more than he seeks.

—John Muir

Into nature we go and what can we find,
so many critters in their daily lives.

As the sun begins to fill the sky,
a warrior hawk doing a flyby.

A playful deer in the meadow
dancing gracefully with its shadow.

The social butterflies and bees joining the show
in the field where the wildflowers grow.

A sly orange fox heading back to her den
to feed her hungry litter of ten.

A sparkling school of fish in the stream,
beautifully swimming together as a team.

An eager chipmunk, with her
cheeks so big and round,
bringing nuts back to her burrow in the ground.

A wise old owl sitting up in the tree,
spinning his head around to see.

One more nut!
One more nut, One more nut!

NATURE

A happy bluebird singing his best,
while picking up sticks to build a nest.

A noisy woodpecker drumming his beak,
in hopes to hear his friends speak.

An acrobatic squirrel busy as can be,
swinging nonstop from tree to tree.

As the day winds down and the sun starts to rest,
a mischievous raccoon ventures
out for his next quest.

A grand ole tree in the mighty biome
for all the critters to call their home.

A grand ole tree with its roots so deep,
where the critters feel safe and go fast to sleep.

What will you find when you get out and explore
in this beautiful thing we call nature.

About the Author

Having grown up in Wisconsin most of her life, Nicole Lea Turner had nature in her backyard. As a child, you could find Nicole and her sisters encountering all the critters in her book when looking for an adventure in their backyard, in the creek, or in the woods. She also spent a lot of time with her grandparents up north fishing on the lake, camping in the woods, or learning about living the simple life on her grandpa's farm, which included no running water and an outhouse!

Being a stay-at-home mom and an auntie, Nicole became inspired to start writing because she saw the importance of encouraging children to spend time in nature as much as possible. She saw how the connection to nature nurtures the soul and promotes creativity, curiosity, joy, and inspiration, which is needed to stay grounded and grateful throughout life. She has experienced and witnessed firsthand through her son and nieces the powerful impact of simply being outside.

Nicole lives in Ohio with her husband, son, and dog, Leo. She enjoys animals, the outdoors, traveling, and helping others!